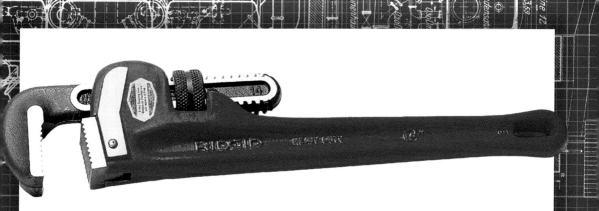

SKILLED TRADE CAREERS
PLUMBERS

by Gary Sprott

Rourke
Educational Media

A Division of
Carson
Dellosa
Education.

Before Reading: *Building Background Knowledge and Vocabulary*

Building background knowledge can help children process new information and build upon what they already know. Before reading a book, it is important to tap into what children already know about the topic. This will help them develop their vocabulary and increase their reading comprehension.

Questions and Activities to Build Background Knowledge:

1. Look at the front cover of the book and read the title. What do you think this book will be about?
2. What do you already know about this topic?
3. Take a book walk and skim the pages. Look at the table of contents, photographs, captions, and bold words. Did these text features give you any information or predictions about what you will read in this book?

Vocabulary: *Vocabulary Is Key to Reading Comprehension*

Use the following directions to prompt a conversation about each word.

- Read the vocabulary words.
- What comes to mind when you see each word?
- What do you think each word means?

Vocabulary Words:
- *apprentice*
- *assemble*
- *clogs*
- *contaminated*
- *unions*
- *wastewater*

During Reading: *Reading for Meaning and Understanding*

To achieve deep comprehension of a book, children are encouraged to use close reading strategies. During reading, it is important to have children stop and make connections. These connections result in deeper analysis and understanding of a book.

Close Reading a Text

During reading, have children stop and talk about the following:

- Any confusing parts
- Any unknown words
- Text to text, text to self, text to world connections
- The main idea in each chapter or heading

Encourage children to use context clues to determine the meaning of any unknown words. These strategies will help children learn to analyze the text more thoroughly as they read.

When you are finished reading this book, turn to the next-to-last page for **After Reading Questions** and an **Activity**.

TABLE OF CONTENTS

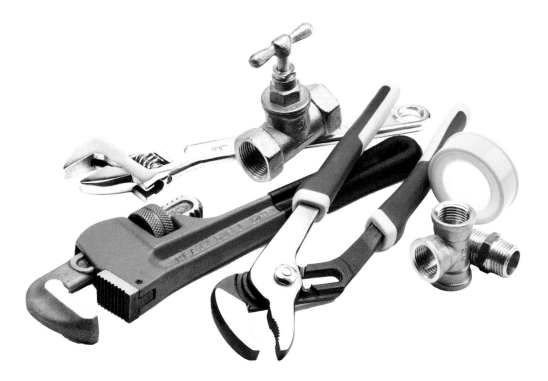

ON THE JOB

Do you like solving puzzles? Does cool technology fascinate you? What about getting your hands dirty? Oh, and how would you like to help save water—one of the planet's most precious resources?

Welcome to a day in the life of a plumber!

A Full Pipeline of Work!

There are about 500,000 plumbers in the United States. That big number is going to get even bigger—jobs for plumbers are growing much faster than most other jobs!

Plumbers use their minds and their muscles on the job.

Plumbing systems are one of the first things to be installed on construction sites.

Plumbers **assemble** pipes to carry gases, water, and other liquids to and from homes, offices, factories, and other buildings. They also install toilets, dishwashers, sinks, and showers. Plumbers use special equipment to find and fix problems such as leaks.

assemble (uh-SEM-buhl): to put together the parts of something

Plumbing has been around for thousands of years! In ancient Rome, fresh water was carried into towns in large structures known as aqueducts. **Wastewater** was piped out through enormous underground sewers. The Romans used lead to make pipes, and that's how plumbers got their name. The Latin word for lead is *plumbum*!

wastewater (wayst-WAW-tur): water after it's used by humans

Pipes of Poison!

Because lead is a soft metal, it was useful for making pipes. But scientists discovered that lead can poison water and make people and animals sick. Many uses of lead are now banned for safety reasons.

The ancient Romans built plumbing to last! Sewer pipes can still be seen centuries after they were last used.

Water can hide many dangerous microorganisms, such as bacteria. That is why having safe, clean drinking water is so important.

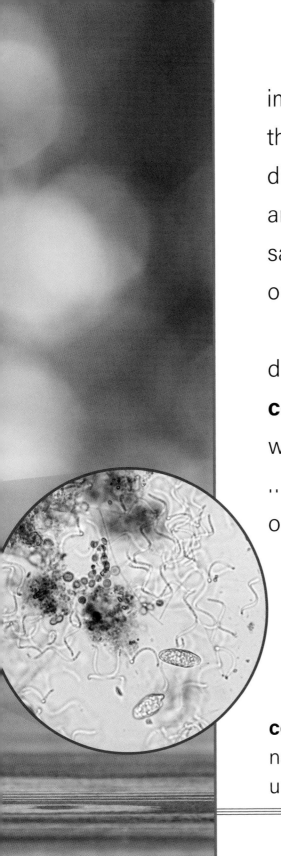

Plumbers play an important role in stopping the spread of deadly diseases, such as typhoid and dysentery. They set up sanitation systems that keep our water clean and safe.

They make sure our drinking water isn't **contaminated** by the dirty water and ... well, other stuff ... that goes down the drain or is flushed down the toilet!

contaminated (kuhn-TAM-uh-nay-tid): containing harmful or undesirable substances

Plumbers don't just protect our health—they also protect the environment! Leaky toilets, faucets, and showers can add up to 10,000 gallons (37,854 liters) of water wasted each year in an average home. Splish, splash! That's enough water to fill about 125 bathtubs!

Many leaks are easy to fix. Stopping the drip can lower your family's water bill.

WHAT'S IN MY TOOLBOX?

Tiny digital cameras. Mechanical snakes! Wireless noise detectors. Soft, sticky putty for watertight seals. Wrenches that grip like gorillas!

A plumber's toolbox is full of cool equipment and supplies for every type of task.

Plumbers are often called for emergency repairs. They need their tools ready at all times.

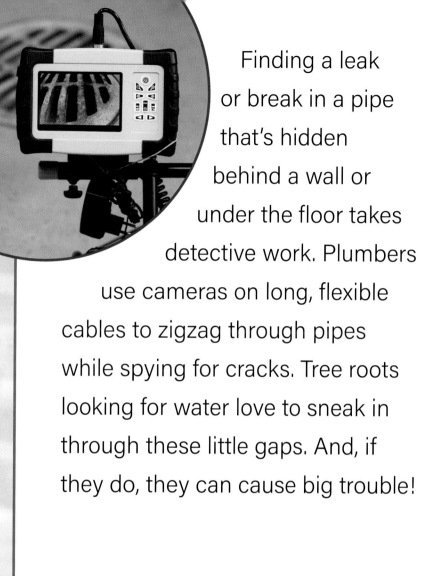

Finding a leak or break in a pipe that's hidden behind a wall or under the floor takes detective work. Plumbers use cameras on long, flexible cables to zigzag through pipes while spying for cracks. Tree roots looking for water love to sneak in through these little gaps. And, if they do, they can cause big trouble!

Hey, You Hear Something?

Acoustic leak detectors can pick up tiny noises like big-eared bats. Plumbers use these powerful microphones to pinpoint the telltale drip, drip, drip in pipes buried deep underground.

Oops, there goes that plastic toy! Ever flushed something down the toilet by mistake? Yup, it happens—and it can cause a huge mess!

A plumber's snake to the rescue! This motorized cable slithers along pipes to clear **clogs**.

clogs (klahgs): objects or materials that block the flow of something

A snake's long, strong cable can clear blockages where a plumber's arm can't reach.

LEARNING THE TRADE

How do you become a plumber? Well, first of all, you need to study hard in school! This skilled trade career usually requires at least a high school diploma.

After graduating, would-be plumbers might head to a technical college or become an **apprentice**.

apprentice (uh-PREN-tis): someone who learns a skill by working with an expert

High school students learn how to safely use plumbing tools.

Details, details! Plumbers make sure that measurements are spot-on and connections are watertight.

Plumbers need a mix of skills and knowledge to succeed. Math, physics, and chemistry are musts for reading plans, calculating angles, and understanding how liquids and gases act. See, you will use all that math and science you learned in school!

Flushing Out Danger!

Proper plumbing keeps people healthy and helps the planet. Bad plumbing? It's dangerous! That's why plumbers must know safety laws and environmental rules.

Apprentice plumbers spend several years working alongside experienced professionals. This way, they can earn a living while learning the ins and outs of the trade. It's kind of like learning to ride a bike with training wheels and a hand holding the seat!

After completing an apprenticeship, plumbers are ready to work on their own.

Master plumbers are experienced professionals who have passed an exam.

Apprenticeships and other training programs are offered by **unions**. These groups of workers organize to negotiate for better pay and working conditions. The United Association has been supporting and training plumbers since 1889. That's years before many homes in the U.S. even had indoor plumbing!

unions (YOON-yuhns): organized groups of workers set up to help improve wages, working conditions, and health benefits

The life of a plumber can be an around-the-clock challenge. Sink overflowing in the middle of the night? Call a plumber! Remember, for this trade, you'll need more than just skilled hands—you'll need some big-time brainpower!

A Superhero with a Wrench?

Did you know that one of the world's most popular video games starred … wait for it … plumbers? Mario and Luigi, better known as the Super Mario Brothers, battled creatures creeping out of the sewers of New York City!

MEMORY GAME

Look at the pictures. What do you remember reading on the pages where each image appeared?

INDEX

AFTER READING QUESTIONS

1. How many plumbers are there in the United States?
2. Name three things that plumbers install.
3. How did plumbers get their name?
4. Why do plumbers use a snake?
5. How do unions help plumbers?

ACTIVITY

Plumbers help conserve water by fixing leaks and installing special equipment. Can you think of five ways your family could save water? How about while taking a shower or bath? Or while doing dishes? Write your ideas.

ABOUT THE AUTHOR

Gary Sprott is a writer in Tampa, Florida. He has written books about ancient cultures, plants, animals, and automobiles. He's also written books about snakes—the scary, venomous kind, not the ones used by plumbers!

www.rourkeeducationalmedia.com

PHOTO CREDITS: Cover: ©DenBoma; Cover: ©artisteer; page 1: ©TheAdcomGroup / Wikimedia; page 1: ©xresch / Pixabay; page 3: ©ifong / shutterstock.com; page 4: ©Phovoir / shutterstock.com; page 5: ©Monkey Business Images / shutterstock.com; page 6: ©Chinnabanchon9Job / shutterstock.com; page 8: ©Eduardo Estellez / shutterstock.com; page 9: ©Volodymyr Baleha / shutterstock.com; page 10: ©Alter-ego / shutterstock.com; page 11: ©Rattiya Thongdumhyu / shutterstock.com; page 12: ©Jazmine Thomas / shutterstock.com; page 13: ©FotoDuets / shutterstock.com; page 14: ©kurhan / shutterstock.com; page 15: ©visivastudio / shutterstock.com; page 16: ©mikeledray / shutterstock.com; page 17: ©JRJfin / shutterstock.com; page 19: ©David Spates / shutterstock.com; page 21: ©Monkey Business Images / shutterstock.com; page 22: ©kurhan / shutterstock.com; page 23: ©Lisa F. Young / shutterstock.com; page 25: ©Monkey Business Images / shutterstock.com; page 26: ©goodluz / shutterstock.com; page 28: ©enchanted_fairy / shutterstock.com; page 29: ©Jovica Varga / shutterstock.com;

Edited by: Madison Capitano
Cover design by: Rhea Magaro-Wallace
Interior design by: Book Buddy Media

Library of Congress PCN Data

Plumbers / Gary Sprott
(Skilled Trade Careers)
    ISBN 978-1-73163-830-4 (hard cover)
    ISBN 978-1-73163-907-3 (soft cover)
    ISBN 978-1-73163-984-4 (e-Book)
    ISBN 978-1-73164-061-1 (e-Pub)
Library of Congress Control Number: 2020930261

Rourke Educational Media
Printed in the United States of America
01-1662011937